唐可儿奇遇记

SUGAR-LOAF MOUNTAIN
糖块山

【美】莱曼·弗兰克·鲍姆 著

【美】梅金尼尔·恩赖特 绘

马爱农 译　　晓 华 + Emma 朗读

中国国际广播出版社

让优秀的双语桥梁书
引领孩子进入英语文学世界
（代序）

晓华

　　《唐可儿奇遇记》是美国儿童文学家弗兰克·鲍姆（L. Frank Baum）所著的另一隐秘的奇幻佳作，风靡西方百年后，首次在中国面世。作为《绿野仙踪》的作者，鲍姆在中国可算是大名鼎鼎，但知道或读过《唐可儿奇遇记》的人却并不多。

　　弗兰克·鲍姆是位极为高产的作家。他一生写过六十二本书，大多数都是为孩子写的，其中光是由《绿野仙踪》的故事延伸出来的奥兹国系列小说就有十四本，此外还有不少书，其中的人物多与奥兹国有关。

《唐可儿奇遇记》是一个完全独立的童话故事系列，以生活在草原小镇上的小姑娘唐可儿为主角，讲述了她在动物世界的神奇冒险。与《绿野仙踪》中的多萝西一样，唐可儿活泼大胆、心直口快，并且，据说这两个人物的原型，其实是同一个人，都是鲍姆妻子的外甥女玛格达雷娜。玛格达雷娜一家住在达科他草原的埃奇利小镇上，鲍姆笔下的唐可儿也住在埃奇利小镇。而多萝西的家乡虽然在堪萨斯，可《绿野仙踪》中描写的她家周围的环境，与达科他草原其实并无二致。

　　有意思的是，在《唐可儿奇遇记》首次出版时，鲍姆并没有署自己的名字，而是使用了笔名 Laura Bancroft。鲍姆的大量作品都使用了不同的笔名，有人说这是因为他太能写了，用笔名是不想市面上同时出现太多部他写的书，互相之间形成竞争。不过，也许是因为这套小说出版之后卖得太好，又或许是鲍姆认为这一系列和《绿野仙踪》一样都是自己的得意之作，到《唐可儿奇遇记》再版的时候，他就又署回了本名，弗兰克·鲍姆。

《唐可儿奇遇记》系列包括六本小说，此次中国国际广播出版社带给读者的是其中的三本。《唐可儿梦游仙境》主要讲述了唐可儿去大峡谷采蓝莓，她不听甲壳虫的警告，越过了那条魔法线，遇到了能说会动的石头；喜欢吃奶油的蝴蝶；跑得飞快的书本以及故弄玄虚的黄鼠狼等奇妙的现象，并受邀参加舞会的故事。《糖块山》中的故事，则是在潜移默化中帮助孩子了解社会层次，两个孩子无意中进入神秘的城市，在其中遇上各色人群，应付审问和意外，还见证假冒的贵族如何身份败露以及焦虑的公主如何保住地位。《解救泥龟王子》的故事梗概是，唐可儿在小溪边玩耍时抓住了一只会说话的泥龟，经过一番冒险之后，帮助它变回了仙境王子。

　　《唐可儿奇遇记》中的故事传达出的，是人和动物间相互尊重、和谐相处的讯息。比如，在《土拨鼠先生》中，鲍姆借着土拨鼠先生之口，说出了这样一段话："你们残忍地对待可怜的动物，而他们不过是别无他法，找不到吃的就得饿死。其实广阔的田野上生长的东西足够人类和我们都吃的。"

在鲍姆看来，人类按照自己的利益划分动物好坏，进而铲除"坏动物"的行为，实在是一种残忍。

青蛙吃蚊子，所以需要保护；蝗虫吃庄稼，于是需要消灭。在大人们的世界里，按照自己的利益来划分动物是有益还是有害并没有什么不妥。可孩子们不一定这样看。他们对自然世界的尊重，似乎已经超越了我们。前几天，我和女儿Emma在小区散步时，发现一只长尾长身的鼠族动物在马路上一蹿而过。我心里一阵硌硬，正想把过街老鼠的成语解释给她听，她却嚷道："啊！好可爱的大老鼠！"说得我无言以对。也许，像《唐可儿奇遇记》这样以自然和动物为题材的童话故事，之所以受到孩子们的喜爱，正是因为这些故事跳出了一般大人们那狭隘的善恶观吧。

《唐可儿奇遇记》系列是鲍姆专为年龄较小的读者写的章节书，文字上比《绿野仙踪》更简单，也更短小精悍，适合八岁以上、英语水平较好的孩子独立阅读。从亲子阅读到独立阅读，是一个了不起的跨越，也是养成阅读兴趣和习惯的关键期。孩子从依偎在父母身边聆听、翻看绘本，到独自探索英文文字的世界，这期间，寻找到合适的阅读内容对他们至关重要。专门为大孩子而写的章节书，可以说是一个完美的过渡。章节书在词汇、句子长度和内容方面都照顾到年轻读者的需求，篇幅比绘本长了许多，插图减少了，但是故事分成了一个个短章节，一天看不完没关系，夹上书签，把书放在枕边，第二天接着看就好了。

我特别遗憾自己在少年时期没能接触到这样的章节书。在原版英文读物并不丰富的年代，我的英文阅读之旅，从《新概念英语》开始，一下就蹦到了《简爱》《荆棘鸟》之类的经典小说。这些大部头不光生词多，深刻程度也超出我的理解范围，导致我不得不跳过大段大段的描写。直到现在我看原版小说还有个坏习惯，就是看不大进去风景描写，一味贪图情节发展。章节书，对于循序渐进的阅读，对于培养良好的阅读习惯，真是太重要了。

《唐可儿奇遇记》系列的英文版每个故事大约四五千字，分为八个章节，也就是说每一章只有七百个字左右，再加上每本书都配有十几张精美的彩页插图，孩子们读起来一定不会觉得累。书的排版上也充分照顾到孩子们，中英双语分段排版，遇到不认识的字词可以迅速查到中文。如果读得累了，还可以听一听我和女儿Emma录制的双语朗读版，用耳朵享受大师的经典之作。其实听书，也是一种重要的语言学习方式。不管孩子还是大人，在阅读有一定难度的文字时，是不是都特别希望有人能读给自己听？这是因为，听书时眼睛得到了解放，并且，优美的朗读，可以使人更容易进入到文字描绘出的情境中去。

　　在各类儿童英文读物已经很丰富的当下，为孩子选择经典佳作显得尤为重要。一套好的作品，会引领孩子进入英语文学的殿堂。而好书不会被时间埋没。我相信，弗兰克·鲍姆的这套《唐可儿奇遇记》，一百年后仍然会焕发光彩，受到中国孩子们的喜爱。

目录
List of Chapters

I

金钥匙
The Golden Key

02

II

穿过地道
Through the Tunnel

14

III

糖块城
Sugar-Loaf City

26

IV

去国王的宫殿
To the King's Palace

38

V

萨卡琳公主
Princess Sakareen

54

VI

皇家马车
The Royal Chariot

68

VII

唐可儿渴了
Twinkle Gets Thirsty

78

VIII

经历失控后
After the Runaway

92

第一章
Chapter 1

金钥匙
The Golden Key

唐可儿来看望她的老朋友查宾斯，查宾斯的妈妈目前在阿肯色州奥扎克山脚下的一个小镇里教书。唐可儿自己的家是在达科他，因此，此刻周围巍峨的群山令她惊异得睁大了眼睛。

　　糖块山就在附近——实际上非常近，唐可儿简直以为自己一伸胳膊就能够到——又大又圆，高耸入云。再往南一点是脊梁山，再往前去，是一座名叫水晶山的高峰。

TWINKLE had come to visit her old friend Chubbins, whose mother was now teaching school in a little town at the foot of the Ozark Mountains, in Arkansas. Twinkle's own home was in Dakota, so the mountains that now towered around her made her open her eyes in wonder.

Near by—so near, in fact, that she thought she might almost reach out her arm and touch it—was Sugar-Loaf Mountain, round and high and big. And a little to the south was Backbone Mountain, and still farther along a peak called Crystal Mountain.

唐可儿刚到这儿的第二天，就请查宾斯带她去看大山。男孩年纪跟她差不多大，让妈妈给他们准备了一个篮子，里面装满了好吃的东西。然后，他们就出发了，手拉着手，到山坡上去探险。

　　唐可儿没想到去糖块山的路这么远，当来到那个大山包的脚下时，两人都走得很累了。乱石嶙峋的山坡上覆盖着灌木丛和小树。

The very next day after her arrival Twinkle asked Chubbins to take her to see the mountain; and so the boy, who was about her own age, got his mother to fill for them a basket of good things to eat, and away they started, hand in hand, to explore the mountain-side.

It was farther to Sugar-Loaf Mountain than Twinkle had thought, and by the time they reached the foot of the great mound, the rocky sides of which were covered with bushes and small trees, they were both rather tired by the walk.

唐可儿和查宾斯

Twinkle and Chubbins

"我们吃点东西吧。"查宾斯提议道。

"好啊。"唐可儿说。

他们往山上爬了一点，看到几块扁平的大岩石，于是坐在一块青石板上，一边休息，一边吃三明治和蛋糕。

"为什么管它叫'糖块山'呢？"小姑娘抬头望着高高的山顶，问道。

"Let's eat something," suggested Chubbins.

"I'm willing," said Twinkle.

So they climbed up a little way, to where some big rocks lay flat upon the mountain, and sat themselves down upon a slab of rock while they rested and ate some of the sandwiches and cake.

"Why do they call it 'Sugar-Loaf'?" asked the girl, looking far up to the top of the mountain.

"不知道。"查宾斯回答。

"真是个奇怪的名字。"唐可儿若有所思地说。

"是啊,"男孩说,"没准他们也会叫它'姜饼山''矿盐山''茶饼山'呢。人们给山起的名字都挺滑稽,是不是?"

"好像是的。"唐可儿说。

"I don't know," replied Chubbins.

"It's a queer name," said Twinkle, thoughtfully.

"That's so," agreed the boy. "They might as well have called it 'gingerbread' or 'rock-salt,' or 'tea-biscuit.' They call mountains funny names, don't they?"

"Seems as if they do," said Twinkle.

他们坐在一块大石板的边缘，把脚放在另一块差不多大的石板上休息。这些石头似乎在这里好几个世纪了——就像是几个古代巨人随手把它们扔下，然后便扬长而去，不再理会。然而，就在两个孩子用脚蹬着这块岩石时，沉重的岩石突然开始颤动，随即往下滑去。

"留神！"小姑娘喊道，被石板的挪动吓坏了。"我们会掉下去摔伤的！"

They had been sitting upon the edge of one big flat rock, with their feet resting against another that was almost as large. These rocks appeared to have been there for ages,—as if some big giants in olden days had tossed them carelessly down and then gone away and left them. Yet as the children pushed their feet against this one, the heavy mass suddenly began to tremble and then slide downward.

"Look out!" cried the girl, frightened to see the slab of rock move. "We'll fall and get hurt!"

他们赶紧牢牢地坐在第一块岩石上，也就没有受伤。下面那块大石板也并没有从原来的位置挪动多远。

它只是往下出溜了几英尺。两个孩子看着石板原来所在的地方，发现那儿似乎有一扇小铁门，嵌在下面那个牢固的石头上。正是因为上面的石板挪开了，孩子们才看见了它。

"呀，是一扇门！"唐可儿惊叫道。

But they clung to the rock upon which they sat and met with no harm whatever. Nor did the big slab of stone below them move very far from its original position.

It merely slid downward a few feet, and when they looked at the place where it had been they discovered what seemed to be a small iron door, built into the solid stone underneath, and now shown to their view by the moving of the upper rock.

"Why, it's a door!" exclaimed Twinkle.

查宾斯跪下来，仔细察看那扇门。门上有一个圆环，看上去像门把手。查宾斯把它抓住，拼命地用力拉，可是门一动不动。

"锁着呢，唐可儿。"他说。

"你说门下面会是什么？"唐可儿问。

"或许有宝藏！"查宾斯回答，兴奋得眼睛睁得老大。

Chubbins got down upon his knees and examined the door carefully. There was a ring in it that seemed to be a handle, and he caught hold of it and pulled as hard as he could. But it wouldn't move.

"It's locked, Twink," he said.

"What do you'spose is under it?" she asked.

"Maybe it's a treasure!" answered Chubbins, his eyes big with interest.

"或许有宝藏"

"Maybe It's a Treasure"

"算了，查布，我们反正也拿不到。"讲究实际的唐可儿说，"还是继续爬山吧。"

　　说着，她从石板上滑下来，走近那扇门，就在这时，她的脚碰到了一块小石头，小石头咕噜噜滚下山去。接着唐可儿突然顿住，惊讶地喊了一声，因为就在她踢开的那块石头下面，有一个小小的石洞，他们看见洞里躺着一把小小的金钥匙。

"Well, Chub, we can't get it, anyway," said the practical Twinkle; "so let's climb the mountain."

She got down from her seat and approached the door, and as she did so she struck a small bit of rock with her foot and sent it tumbling down the hill. Then she stopped short with a cry of wonder, for under the stone she had kicked away was a little hole in the rock, and within this they saw a small golden key.

"也许，"唐可儿急切地说，一边俯身去捡钥匙，"这能打开那扇铁门的锁。"

"我们试试吧！"男孩喊道。

"Perhaps," she said, eagerly, as she stooped to pick up the key, "this will unlock the iron door."

"Let's try it!" cried the boy.

第二章
Chapter II

穿过地道
Through the Tunnel

他们对着门仔细端详，终于发现靠近门中间的地方有个小洞。唐可儿把金钥匙插进去，不大不小刚刚好。可是锁生锈了，查宾斯用了吃奶的力气才把钥匙拧动。最后锁打开了，他们听见锁舌弹开的声音，于是两人同时抓住圆环，一起用力，总算把连着铰链的铁门掀了起来。

他们只看见一条黑乎乎的地道，那些石阶一直往下，通向大山深处。

THEY examined the door carefully, and at last found near the center of it a small hole. Twinkle put the golden key into this and found that it fitted exactly. But it took all of Chubbins's strength to turn the key in the rusty lock. Yet finally it did turn, and they heard the noise of bolts shooting back, so they both took hold of the ring, and pulling hard together, managed to raise the iron door on its hinges.

All they saw was a dark tunnel, with stone steps leading down into the mountain.

"没有什么财宝。"小姑娘说。

"也许财宝在更深处，"查宾斯回应，"我们下去吗？"

"会不会有危险？"唐可儿问。

"不知道。"查宾斯实话实说，"这扇门已经很多年、很多年没有打开了。你自己也能看见，那块岩石肯定是很久以前就盖在门上的。"

"No treasure here," said the little girl.

"P'raps it's farther in," replied Chubbins. "Shall we go down?"

"Won't it be dangerous?" she asked.

"Don't know," said Chubbins, honestly. "It's been years and years since this door was opened. You can see for yourself. That rock must have covered it up a long time."

"里面肯定有什么东西，"唐可儿大声说，"不然就不会有门，也不会有台阶。"

"是啊。"查宾斯回答，"我下去看看吧。你在这儿等着。"

"不，我也要下去。"唐可儿说，"我等在外面跟呆在里面一样害怕。而且我比你大，查布。"

"There must be *something* inside," she declared, "or there wouldn't be any door, or any steps."

"That's so," answered Chubbins. "I'll go down and see. You wait."

"No; I'll go too," said Twinkle. "I'd be just as scared waiting outside as I would be in. And I 'in bigger than you are, Chub."

穿过地道
They Enter the Tunnel

"唐可儿，你只是个子高，实际上只比我大一个月；所以别显出了不起的样子。我比你强壮多了。"

"我们俩都进去吧，"唐可儿说，"如果发现了财宝，就两人平分。"

"好，走吧！"

"You're taller, but you're only a month older, Twink; so don't you put on airs. And I'm the strongest."

"We'll both go," she decided; "and then if we find the treasure we'll divide."

"All right; come on!"

他们忘记了放在石板上的篮子，从那个小门洞爬进去，拾阶而下。一共只有七级台阶，然后是一条狭窄却平坦的地道，径直通进山坡深处。离开门几英尺就是漆黑一片，但两个孩子没有退缩。他们手拉着手，以免互相走散，摸索着洞壁，在黑黢黢的地道里走了很久。

Forgetting their basket, which they left upon the rocks, they crept through the little doorway and down the steps. There were only seven steps in all, and then came a narrow but level tunnel that led straight into the mountain-side. It was dark a few feet from the door, but the children resolved to go on. Taking hold of hands, so as not to get separated, and feeling the sides of the passage to guide them, they walked a long way into the black tunnel.

唐可儿刚想说还是返回吧，地道突然拐了个弯，前面远远地闪耀着一道微弱的光。这使两个孩子有了勇气，脚下加快了速度，他们希望很快就能找到财宝。

　　"坚持走下去，唐可儿，"男孩说，"还没必要回家呢。"

　　"我们肯定差不多走到糖块山的中间了。"唐可儿回答。

　　Twinkle was just about to say they'd better go back, when the passage suddenly turned, and far ahead of them shone a faint light. This encouraged them, and they went on faster, hoping they would soon come to the treasure.

　　"Keep it up, Twink," said the boy. "It's no use going home yet."

　　"We must be almost in the middle of Sugar-Loaf Mountain," she answered.

"哦，还没有，这是一座大得吓人的山。"查宾斯说，"但我们确实已经走了很远，是不是？"

"我想，妈妈如果知道我们在哪里，肯定会骂我的。"

"什么也别让妈妈们知道，"查宾斯说，"因为她们只会担心。只要我们别受伤，我就觉得不会有什么危险。"

"Oh, no; it's an awful big mountain," said he. "But we've come quite a way, haven't we?"

"I guess mama'd scold, if she knew where we are."

"Mamas," said Chubbins, "shouldn't know everything, 'cause they'd only worry. And if we don't get hurt I can't see as there's any harm done."

"可是我们不能不听话呀，查布。"

"不听话指的是，别人不让你做的事你偏要做。"查宾斯回答，"并没有人叫我们不要走进糖块山内部来呀。"

"But we mustn't be naughty, Chub."

"The only thing that's naughty," he replied, "is doing what you're told not to do. And no one told us not to go into the middle of Sugar-Loaf Mountain."

就在这时，地道又拐了一个弯，前面出现了一道明亮的光。孩子们觉得那看上去如同白昼。于是他们朝着光芒跑了起来，不一会儿，经过一道低矮的拱门，来到了——

天哪！眼前的景象太奇异了，他们惊讶得差点儿喘不过气来，一动不动地站在那儿，瞪着大眼睛，使劲地看啊看。

Just then they came to another curve in their path, and saw a bright light ahead. It looked to the children just like daylight; so they ran along and soon passed through a low arch and came out into—

Well! The scene before them was so strange that it nearly took away their breath, and they stood perfectly still and stared as hard as their big eyes could possibly stare.

奇异的景象

The Scene was Strange

第三章
Chapter III

糖块城
Sugar-Loaf City

糖块山里面是空的，两个孩子面前是一个硕大的穹顶，看上去简直像天空一样高。穹顶下面，是一座任何人所能想象的最美丽的城市。有房屋，有街道，有圆顶的建筑，有修长精美、高耸入云的尖塔，还有装饰着石雕的美丽角楼。所有这些都洁白如雪，每一处都像镶着几百万颗钻石一样闪闪发光——因为这里的一切都是用毫无杂质的纯糖块做的！

SUGAR-LOAF Mountain was hollow inside, for the children stood facing a great dome that rose so far above their heads that it seemed almost as high as the sky. And underneath this dome lay spread out the loveliest city imaginable. There were streets of houses, and buildings with round domes, and slender, delicate spires reaching far up into the air, and turrets beautifully ornamented with carvings. And all these were white as the driven snow and sparkling in every part like millions of diamonds—for all were built of pure loaf-sugar!

街上的人行道也是糖块铺成，树、灌木和鲜花同样也是糖，但那些花不是全白，因为糖并不都是白的，而是展现出各种鲜艳的颜色，有红糖、蓝糖、黄糖、紫糖和绿糖，它们都和晶莹闪烁的白色建筑以及头上宏伟的白色穹顶，形成了极其美丽的反差。

The pavements of the streets were also loaf-sugar, and the trees and bushes and flowers were likewise sugar; but these last were not all white, because all sugar is not white, and they showed many bright colors of red sugar and blue sugar and yellow, purple and green sugar, all contrasting most prettily with the sparkling white buildings and the great white dome overhead.

对于这两个来自外部世界的孩子，这幕景象已经够令人吃惊的了，但唐可儿和查宾斯第一次用好奇的目光打量糖块城时，看见的还不止这些呢。城里还居住着许多人——男人、女人和孩子——他们走在街道上，步履跟我们一样轻快，只是所有的人都是糖做的。

This alone might well astonish the eyes of children from the outside world, but it was by no means all that Twinkle and Chubbins beheld in that first curious look at Sugar-Loaf City. For the city was inhabited by many people—men, women and children—who walked along the streets just as briskly as we do; only all were made of sugar.

这些糖人分为几个不同种类。有的走起路来趾高气扬，显然是纯糖块做的，一副尊贵显赫的样子；另一些像是用浅褐色的糖做成，举手投足比较谦卑，走路匆匆忙忙，似乎手头有事情要办；还有一些糖人的颜色非常深，唐可儿怀疑是枫糖做的，地位似乎比别人更低，都是些仆人、马车夫、乞丐和游手好闲之辈。

There were several different kinds of these sugar people. Some, who strutted proudly along, were evidently of pure loaf-sugar, and these were of a most respectable appearance. Others seemed to be made of a light brown sugar, and were more humble in their manners and seemed to hurry along as if they had business to attend to. Then there were some of sugar so dark in color that Twinkle suspected it was maple-sugar, and these folks seemed of less account than any of the others, being servants, drivers of carriages, and beggars and idlers.

"投降！"队长喊道

"Surrender!" Said the Captain

在街道上行进的板车和马车，大多都是红糖做的。拉车的马要么是榨糖，要么是枫糖。实际上，在这个奇妙的城市里，所有的一切都是不同种类的糖做成的。

这么明亮、美丽的一个地方，光是从哪儿来的呢？唐可儿想象不出。这儿没有太阳，也看不见任何电灯，却像大白天一样明亮，每样东西都能看得清清楚楚。

Carts and carriages moved along the streets, and were mostly made of brown sugar. The horses that drew them were either pressed sugar or maple-sugar. In fact, everything that existed in this wonderful city was made of some kind of sugar.

Where the light, which made all this place so bright and beautiful, came from, Twinkle could not imagine. There was no sun, nor were there any electric lights that could be seen; but it was fully as bright as day and everything showed with great plainness.

孩子们站在刚才通过的那道拱门下，打量着糖块城的种种奇观，突然，一队糖兵从拐角那儿迅速地跑了过来。

"立定！"队长喊道。他穿着一件红色的糖外衣，戴着一顶红色的糖帽子；士兵们的穿戴跟队长一样，但是没有黄糖做的军官肩章。听到命令，糖兵们停下脚步，都把手里的糖火枪对准了唐可儿和查宾斯。

While the children, who stood just inside the archway through which they had entered, were looking at the wonders of Sugar-Loaf City, a file of sugar soldiers suddenly came around a corner at a swift trot.

"Halt!" cried the Captain. He wore a red sugar jacket and a red sugar cap, and the soldiers were dressed in the same manner as their Captain, but without the officer's yellow sugar shoulder-straps. At the command, the sugar soldiers came to a stop, and all pointed their sugar muskets at Twinkle and Chubbins.

"投降！"队长朝两个孩子喊道，"快投降，不然我就——我就——"

他迟疑着。

"你就怎么样呢？"唐可儿说。

"我也不知道，但肯定非常可怕。"队长回答，"不过你们肯定会投降的。"

"Surrender!" said the Captain to them. "Surrender, or I'll—I'll—"

He hesitated.

"What will you do?" said Twinkle.

"I don't know what, but something very dreadful," replied the Captain. "But of course you'll surrender."

"我想我们不得不投降。"小姑娘回答。

"这就对了。我要带你们去见国王，让他决定该怎么做。"队长愉快地加了一句。

于是士兵们把两个孩子围在中间，扛起武器，大踏步地在街上走，唐可儿和查宾斯走得很慢，这样那些糖人就用不着跑步，要知道，那个最高的士兵也只齐到他们的肩膀呢。

"I suppose we'll have to," answered the girl.

"That's right. I'll just take you to the king, and let him decide what to do," he added pleasantly.

So the soldiers surrounded the two children, shouldered arms, and marched away down the street, Twinkle and Chubbins walking slowly, so the candy folks would not have to run; for the tallest soldiers were only as high as their shoulders.

　　"这可是一件大事儿，"队长说，他端足架子，煞有介事地走在两个孩子身边，"你们能到这儿来被逮捕真是太好了，我已经很长时间没遇到什么兴奋的事儿了。这里的人都是规规矩矩的糖，很少做什么坏事。"

　　"This is a great event," remarked the Captain, as he walked beside them with as much dignity as he could muster. "It was really good of you to come and be arrested, for I haven't had any excitement in a long time. The people here are such good sugar that they seldom do anything wrong."

两个孩子和队长对话

The Children Talk to the Captain

第四章
Chapter IV

去国王的宫殿
To the King's Palace

"请允许我问一句，你们是哪个等级的糖？"队长非常礼貌地问，"看上去不像顶级糖块，但我相信你们肯定是实心的。"

"实心的什么？"查宾斯问。

"实心的糖。"队长回答。

"我们根本不是糖，"唐可儿解释说，"就是肉。"

"WHAT, allow me to ask, is your grade of sugar?" inquired the Captain, with much politeness. "You do not seem to be the best loaf, but I suppose that of course you are solid."

"Solid what?" asked Chubbins.

"Solid sugar," replied the Captain.

"We're not sugar at all," explained Twinkle. "We're just meat."

"肉！肉是什么？"

"你们城里没有肉吗？"

"没有。"队长摇摇头答道。

"嗯，我也解释不清肉到底是什么，"唐可儿说，"反正不是糖。"

听了这话，队长的神情变得严肃起来。

"Meat! And what is that?"

"Haven't you any meat in your city?"

"No," he replied, shaking his head.

"Well, I can't explain exactly what meat is," she said; "but it isn't sugar, anyway."

At this the Captain looked solemn.

"说到底，这件事跟我无关。"他对两个孩子说，"怎么处理你们，必须由国王决定，那是归他负责的。但既然你们不是糖做的，就必须原谅我不再愿意与你们交谈了，那么做有失我的身份。"

"噢，没关系。"唐可儿说。

"在我们那个地方，"查宾斯说，"肉比糖贵得多，所以我猜我们的品质并不比你差。"

"It isn't any of my business, after all," he told them. "The king must decide about you, for that's *his* business. But since you are not made of sugar you must excuse me if I decline to converse with you any longer. It is beneath my dignity."

"Oh, that's all right," said Twinkle.

"Where we came from," said Chubbins, "meat costs more a pound than sugar does; so I guess we're just as good as you are."

可是队长听了这话没有回答，不一会儿，他们就停在了一座糖做的大厦前，一大群糖人迅速聚集过来。

"往后站站！"队长喊道，糖兵们在两个孩子和糖民们之间排成一队，不让人群靠得太近。然后，队长领着唐可儿和查宾斯穿过一道高高的糖门，顺着一条宽阔的糖路，走向大厦的正门。

But the Captain made no reply to this statement, and before long they stopped in front of a big sugar building, while a crowd of sugar people quickly gathered.

"Stand back!" cried the Captain, and the sugar soldiers formed a row between the children and the sugar citizens, and kept the crowd from getting too near. Then the Captain led Twinkle and Chubbins through a high sugar gateway and up a broad sugar walk to the entrance of the building.

"这一定是国王的城堡。"查宾斯说。

"是国王的宫殿。"队长用硬邦邦的口气纠正道。

"有什么区别吗?"唐可儿问。

可是糖兵队长根本不屑于解释。

"Must be the king's castle," said Chubbins.

"The king's palace," corrected the Captain, stiffly.

"What's the difference?" asked Twinkle.

But the sugar officer did not care to explain.

国王的宫殿

The King's Palace

红糖做的仆人，穿着紫红色的糖衣，站在宫殿门口，看见队长领来了两个陌生人，他们的眼睛像圆糖片一样，从他们的糖脸上突了出来。

每个仆人都深鞠一躬，闪身让他们通过，他们走过一间间美丽的大厅和会客室，在这些地方，糖块被切割成镶板和涡纹，还雕刻成各种各样的水果和鲜花。

Brown sugar servants in plum-colored sugar coats stood at the entrance to the palace, and their eyes stuck out like lozenges from their sugar faces when they saw the strangers the Captain was escorting.

But every one bowed low, and stood aside for them to pass, and they walked through beautiful halls and reception rooms where the sugar was cut into panels and scrolls and carved to represent all kinds of fruit and flowers.

"是不是很可爱！"唐可儿说。

"那还用说。"查宾斯回答。

此刻他们被领进了一个富丽堂皇的房间，有一个结结实实的小糖人，正坐在窗户旁边拉小提琴；一群糖做的男人女人毕恭毕敬地站在他面前，听他拉琴。

"Isn't it sweet!" said Twinkle.

"Sure it is," answered Chubbins.

And now they were ushered into a magnificent room, where a stout little sugar man was sitting near the window playing upon a fiddle, while a group of sugar men and women stood before him in respectful attitudes and listened to the music.

唐可儿立刻便知道，拉琴的就是国王，因为他脑袋上戴着一顶糖王冠。国王陛下的身体是用洁白无瑕、晶莹剔透的糖块做成的，身上的衣服也是同样纯粹的材质。他全身唯一的色彩，是面颊上的粉红色糖和眼睛里的褐色糖。小提琴也是白糖做的，琴弦是糖丝，音质非常优美。

Twinkle knew at once that the fiddler was the king, because he had a sugar crown upon his head. His Majesty was made of very white and sparkling cut loaf-sugar, and his clothing was formed of the same pure material. The only color about him was the pink sugar in his cheeks and the brown sugar in his eyes. His fiddle was also of white sugar, and the strings were of spun sugar and had an excellent tone.

国王看见两个陌生的孩子走进房间，惊讶得跳了起来，喊道："我的老天爷啊！来的这是谁呀？"

"是凡人，最晶莹、最结实的国王陛下。"队长说着，深深地鞠躬，额头都触到了地面。"他们是从那条古地道进来的。"

"啊，我要声明，"国王说，"我还以为那条地道永远被封死了呢。"

When the king saw the strange children enter the room he jumped up and exclaimed: "Bless my beets! What have we here?"

"Mortals, Most Granular and Solidified Majesty," answered the Captain, bowing so low that his forehead touched the floor. "They came in by the ancient tunnel."

"Well, I declare," said the king. "I thought that tunnel had been stopped up for good and all."

"门上的那块石头滑落了，"唐可儿说，"所以我们就下来看看能发现什么。"

"你们千万别再这么做了。"国王陛下严厉地说，"这是我们的专属王国，一个安宁而幽静的民族，由特别精致而有质感的臣民组成，我们不希望与凡人或其他人打交道。"

"我们很快就会回去的。"唐可儿说。

"The stone above the door slipped," said Twinkle, "so we came down to see what we could find."

"You must never do it again," said his Majesty, sternly. "This is our own kingdom, a peaceful and retired nation of extra refined and substantial citizens, and we don't wish to mix with mortals, or any other folks."

"We'll go back, pretty soon," said Twinkle.

尊贵的国王陛下

His Majesty the King

"啊，那可真是太好了。"国王大声说，"我感谢你们的好意。亲爱的，你们是特别精致的吗？"

"但愿吧。"小姑娘有点不敢肯定地说。

"那么，在你们逗留期间我们表现得友好一点倒也无妨。既然你保证很快就会返回你们自己的世界，我不反对带你们到城里各处转转。你们肯定愿意看看我们是怎么生活的，是不是？"

"Now, that's very nice of you," declared the king, "and I appreciate your kindness. Are you extra refined, my dear?"

"I hope so," said the girl, a little doubtfully.

"Then there's no harm in our being friendly while you're here. And as you've promised to go back to your own world soon, I have no objection to showing you around the town. You'd like to see how we live, wouldn't you?"

"非常愿意。"唐可儿说。

"吩咐备好我的马车，脆脆队长。"国王陛下说。于是队长又深鞠一躬，趾高气扬地走出房间，执行命令去了。

这时，国王把查宾斯和唐可儿介绍给了在场的糖贵妇和糖绅士，他们都对两个孩子表现得十分尊敬。

"Very much," said Twinkle.

"Order my chariot, Captain Brittle," said his Majesty; and the Captain again made one of his lowly bows and strutted from the room to execute the command.

The king now introduced Chubbins and Twinkle to the sugar ladies and gentlemen who were present, and all of them treated the children very respectfully.

第五章
Chapter V

萨卡琳公主
Princess Sakareen

"喂，给我们拉个曲子吧。"查宾斯对国王说。国王陛下似乎不喜欢别人这么不客气地对他说话，但他非常喜欢拉琴，就宽容地答应了查宾斯的央求，在那些糖丝上拉了一首优美而感伤的歌谣。然后，趁马车还没有备好，国王请求原谅他离开几分钟，出门去了另一个房间。

"SAY, play us a tune," said Chubbins to the king. His Majesty didn't seem to like being addressed so bluntly, but he was very fond of playing the fiddle, so he graciously obeyed the request and played a pretty and pathetic ballad upon the spun sugar strings. Then, begging to be excused for a few minutes while the chariot was being made ready, the king left them and went into another room.

这使两个孩子有机会跟那些糖人自由地交谈。查宾斯对一个外表看上去非常光滑的男人说道：

　　"我猜想你准是这里的大人物，对吗？"

　　男人一时间似乎有点惶恐，随即拉着男孩的胳膊，把他领到房间的角落里。

This gave the children a chance to talk freely with the sugar people, and Chubbins said to one man, who looked very smooth on the outside:

"I s'pose you're one of the big men of this place, aren't you?"

The man looked frightened for a moment, and then took the boy's arm and led him into a corner of the room.

"你问了一个令我尴尬的问题。"男人小声说，一边四处张望，确保没有人听见他说话，"我虽然装出一副贵族的派头，但实际上，我是一个大骗子！"

"怎么回事儿？"查宾斯问。

"你注意到我有多么光滑吗？"糖人问。

"注意到了，"男孩回答，"为什么会这样？"

"You ask me an embarrassing question," he whispered, looking around to make sure that no one overheard. "Although I pose as one of the nobility, I am, as a matter of fact, a great fraud!"

"How's that?" asked Chubbins.

"Have you noticed how smooth I am?" inquired the sugar man.

"Yes," replied the boy. "Why is it?"

"我装出一副贵族的派头"

"I Pose as One of the Nobility"

"唉，原因就是，我裹了一层糖霜。这里没有人对此表示怀疑，都认为我非常值得尊敬。但事情的真相是，我只是外面包了一层糖霜，根本不是实心糖做的。"

"那你身体里是什么？"查宾斯问。

"这个，"男人回答，"我也不知道，我从来不敢弄清楚。如果我打破糖霜，看看里面塞了什么，别人也都会看到，我就会名誉扫地，彻底完蛋了。"

"Why, I'm frosted, that's the reason. No one here suspects it, and I'm considered very respectable; but the truth is, I'm just coated over with frosting, and not solid sugar at all."

"What's inside you?" asked Chubbins.

"That," answered the man, "I do not know. I've never dared to find out. For if I broke my frosting to see what I'm stuffed with, every one else would see too, and I would be disgraced and ruined."

"也许你是蛋糕。"男孩提议道。

"也许是的。"男人回答，语气忧伤。"请替我保守秘密，在这个国家，只有那些实心糖块做成的才有身份。目前，你也看见了，我被上流社会所接纳。"

"哦，我不会说的。"查宾斯说。

"Perhaps you're cake," suggested the boy.

"Perhaps so," answered the man, sadly. "Please keep my secret, for only those who are solid loaf-sugar are of any account in this country, and at present I am received in the best society, as you see."

"Oh, I won't tell," said Chubbins.

与此同时，唐可儿一直在房间的另一边，跟一个糖贵妇聊天。这位女士看上去像是毫无杂质的纯糖块做的，晶莹剔透、光彩照人，唐可儿简直可以说她是自己见过的最漂亮的人了。

　　"你是国王的亲戚吗？"唐可儿问。

During this time Twinkle had been talking with a sugar lady, in another part of the room. This lady seemed to be of the purest loaf-sugar, for she sparkled most beautifully, and Twinkle thought she was quite the prettiest person to look at that she had yet seen.

"Are you related to the king?" she asked.

"才不是呢。"糖贵妇回答，"虽然别人都把我看得地位很高，实际上，亲爱的，我告诉你一个秘密吧。"她拉住唐可儿的手，把她领到一张糖沙发前，两人都坐了下来。

"没有一个人，"糖贵妇继续说道，"怀疑到事情的真相：其实我是一个冒牌货，这弄得我整天惶惶不安。"

"No, indeed," answered the sugar lady, "although I'm considered one of the very highest quality. But I'll tell you a secret, my dear." She took Twinkle's hand and led her across to a sugar sofa, where they both sat down.

"No one," resumed the sugar lady, "has ever suspected the truth; but I'm only a sham, and it worries me dreadfully."

"我不明白你的话是什么意思，"唐可儿说，"你身上的糖看上去跟国王的一样闪闪发亮，一点杂质也没有。"

"事情并不总像表面看上去的那样。"糖贵妇叹着气说，"从外表上看，我一切都好；但实际上，我是空心的！"

"天哪！"唐可儿惊呼，"你是怎么知道的呢？"

"I don't understand what you mean," said Twinkle. "Your sugar seems as pure and sparkling as that of the king."

"Things are not always what they seem," sighed the sugar lady. "What you see of me, on the outside, is all right; but the fact is, *I'm hollow*!"

"Dear me!" exclaimed Twinkle, in surprise. "How do you know it?"

"我是空心的！"
"I'm Hollow!"

"我可以感觉到。"贵妇人煞有介事地回答，"你如果给我称称重量，就会发现我不像实心的那么重，我是空心的。这个残酷的事实我已经发现了很长时间。我因此而郁郁寡欢，却又不敢把我的秘密透露给这里的任何人，那会使我永远抬不起头来的。"

"换了我就不会担心，"小姑娘说，"他们永远不会知道有什么不同。"

"I can feel it," answered the lady, impressively. "If you weighed me you'd find I'm not as heavy as the solid ones, and for a long time I've realized the bitter truth that I'm hollow. It makes me very unhappy, but I don't dare confide my secret to any one here, because it would disgrace me forever."

"I wouldn't worry," said the child. "They'll never know the difference."

"除非我有什么破损。"糖贵妇回答，"如果发生那样的事，全世界都会看出我是空心的，到时候我会被上流社会扫地出门，无人理睬。就算是红糖做的，也比空心的更值得尊敬啊，你认为不是吗？"

"我对这里不熟悉，"唐可儿说，"没法做出判断。但如果我是你，就不会操这份心，等有了破损再说呗。而且，你可能弄错了，你没准像砖头一样扎实呢！"

"Not unless I should break," replied the sugar lady. "But if that happened, all the world could see that I'm hollow, and instead of being welcomed in good society I'd become an outcast. It's even more respectable to be made of brown sugar, than to be hollow; don't you think so?"

"I'm a stranger here," said Twinkle; "so I can't judge. But if I were you, I wouldn't worry unless I got broke; and you may be wrong, after all, and as sound as a brick!"

第六章
Chapter VI

皇家马车
The Royal Chariot

就在这时，国王回到房间，说道：

"马车就在门口，车上有三个座位，我们带上克罗伊老爷和萨卡琳公主。"

于是，两个孩子跟着国王走到宫殿门口，那儿有一辆白糖和黄糖做成的美丽的双轮敞篷马车，拉车的是六匹英俊的糖马，尾巴和马鬃都是糖丝做的，红糖赶车人身上穿着一件蓝色的糖制服。

JUST then the king came back to the room and said:

"The chariot is at the door; and, as there are three seats, I'll take Lord Cloy and Princess Sakareen with us."

So the children followed the king to the door of the palace, where stood a beautiful white and yellow sugar chariot, drawn by six handsome sugar horses with spun sugar tails and manes, and driven by a brown sugar coachman in a blue sugar livery.

国王先上了马车，另外两人也跟了上去。孩子们发现，克罗伊老爷就是那个裹糖霜的男人，萨卡琳公主就是那个告诉唐可儿自己是空心的糖贵妇。

一大群糖人聚在宫殿门口，观看皇家马车出发，几个士兵和警察在现场维持秩序。唐可儿坐在国王身边，查宾斯跟萨卡琳公主坐同一个座位，克罗伊老爷只好去跟赶车人合坐。

The king got in first, and the others followed. Then the children discovered that Lord Cloy was the frosted man and Princess Sakareen was the sugar lady who had told Twinkle that she was hollow.

There was quite a crowd of sugar people at the gates to watch the departure of the royal party, and a few soldiers and policemen were also present to keep order. Twinkle sat beside the king, and Chubbins sat on the same seat with the Princess Sakareen, while Lord Cloy was obliged to sit with the coachman.

一切就绪后，赶车人用糖鞭子打了个响鞭（却没有把鞭子甩断），马车就冲上了用糖块铺成的道路。

　　空气清凉宜人，但微风中有一股甜美的气味，这种甜味儿是这古怪的国家特有的。糖鸟儿飞过来飞过去，唱着悦耳动听的歌，国王的马车疾驶过时，几只糖狗冲出来汪汪大叫。

When all were ready the driver cracked a sugar whip (but didn't break it), and away the chariot dashed over a road paved with blocks of cut loaf-sugar.

The air was cool and pleasant, but there was a sweet smell to the breeze that was peculiar to this strange country. Sugar birds flew here and there, singing sweet songs, and a few sugar dogs ran out to bark at the king's chariot as it whirled along.

皇家马车扬长而去

The Chariot Dashed Away

"你们国家没有汽车吗？"小姑娘问。

"没有，"国王回答，"任何需要热量的东西，在这里都要避免，因为热量会使我们融化，在几分钟内毁掉我们的身体。汽车在糖块城属于危险品。"

"它们在别处其实也很危险。"唐可儿说，"你们喂马吃什么？"

"Haven't you any automobiles in your country?" asked the girl.

"No," answered the king. "Anything that requires heat to make it go is avoided here, because heat would melt us and ruin our bodies in a few minutes. Automobiles would be dangerous in Sugar-Loaf City."

"They're dangerous enough anywhere," she said. "What do you feed to your horses?"

"它们吃我们田里生长的一种优质的大麦糖。"国王回答，"你们很快就能看见，因为马车会驶向我的乡村别墅，那儿靠近穹顶的边缘，就在你们进来的拱门对面。"

尽管如此，他们还是先环游了整个城区，国王指给他们看一些公共建筑、剧院、教堂和许多玲珑别致的公园。城市中央有一座高塔，巍峨耸立，直插向高处的穹顶。

"They eat a fine quality of barley-sugar that grows in our fields," answered the king. "You'll see it presently, for we will drive out to my country villa, which is near the edge of the dome, opposite to where you came in."

First, however, they rode all about the city, and the king pointed out the public buildings, and the theaters, and the churches, and a number of small but pretty public parks. And there was a high tower near the center that rose half-way to the dome, it was so tall.

"你们就不担心穹顶有一天会塌下来，把整个城市毁掉吗？"唐可儿问国王。

　　"哦，不担心，"国王回答，"我们从来不考虑这种事情。在你们生活的地方，难道没有穹顶吗？"

　　"有的，"唐可儿说，"天空就是我们的穹顶。"

"Aren't you afraid the roof will cave in some time, and ruin your city?" Twinkle asked the king.

"Oh, no," he answered. "We never think of such a thing. Isn't there a dome over the place where you live?"

"Yes," said Twinkle; "but it's the sky."

"你们不担心它会塌下来吗?"国王问。

"当然不会!"唐可儿回答,想到那情景,忍不住笑了起来。

"这不就得了,我们也是这样。"国王陛下回答,"穹顶是世界上最坚固的东西。"

"Do you ever fear it will cave in?" inquired the king.

"No, indeed!" she replied, with a laugh at the idea.

"Well, it's the same way with us," returned his Majesty. "Domes are the strongest things in all the world."

糖块农场

A Sugar-Loaf Farm

第七章
Chapter VII

唐可儿渴了
Twinkle Gets Thirsty

欣赏过了城市的景色，马车拐进了一条通往乡村的宽阔大马路。不一会儿，他们开始经过大片种着糖玉米的田地，种着糖白菜、糖甜菜和糖土豆的菜园，还有生长着糖李子和糖苹果的果园，以及挂着糖葡萄的藤蔓园。所有的树都是糖，就连草也是糖，草丛中有糖蚂蚱在跳来跳去。实际上查宾斯认为，在糖块山的穹顶下面，没有一样东西不是纯糖做成的——除非事实证明那个糖霜男人的体内是另一种物质。

AFTER they had seen the sights of the city the carriage turned into a broad highway that led into the country, and soon they began to pass fields of sugar corn and gardens of sugar cabbages and sugar beets and sugar potatoes. There were also orchards of sugar plums and sugar apples and vineyards of sugar grapes. All the trees were sugar, and even the grass was sugar, while sugar grasshoppers hopped about in it. Indeed, Chubbins decided that not a speck of anything beneath the dome of Sugar-Loaf Mountain was anything but pure sugar—unless the inside of the frosted man proved to be of a different material.

不久，他们来到了美丽的别墅，都下了马车，跟着糖国王走进那座糖房子。因为提前打了糖电话，吩咐准备了茶点，所以餐桌都已经摆好。他们只需坐在精巧的糖椅子里，由枫糖做的侍者在一旁伺候。

By and by they reached a pretty villa, where they all left the carriage and followed the sugar king into the sugar house. Refreshments had been ordered in advance, over the sugar telephone, so that the dining table was already laid and all they had to do was to sit in the pretty sugar chairs and be waited upon by maple-sugar attendants.

三明治、沙拉、水果和其他许多糖做的点心，盛在糖盘子里送上来。两个孩子发现有些食品做成了薄荷、覆盆子和柠檬的味道，还是跟糖果一样好吃。每个盘子旁边都有一个水晶糖做的杯子，里面是黏稠的糖浆，似乎是唯一可喝的饮品。两个孩子吃了这么多糖，自然就感到口渴。因此，当国王问唐可儿还想要些什么时，唐可儿不假思索地说——"好的，我想喝点水。"

There were sandwiches and salads and fruits and many other sugar things to eat, served on sugar plates; and the children found that some were flavored with winter-green and raspberry and lemon, so that they were almost as good as candies. At each plate was a glass made of crystal sugar and filled with thick sugar syrup, and this seemed to be the only thing to drink. After eating so much sugar the children naturally became thirsty, and when the king asked Twinkle if she would like anything else she answered promptly—*Yes, I'd like a drink of water.*

在场的糖人们立刻发出一片惊恐的窃窃私语。国王把椅子往后一推，似乎非常恼火。

"水！"他惊愕地喊道。

"是啊，"查宾斯回答，"我也想喝点水。我们都渴了。"

国王哆嗦了一下。

At once a murmur of horror arose from the sugar people present, and the king pushed back his chair as if greatly disturbed.

"Water!" he exclaimed, in amazement.

"Sure," replied Chubbins. "I want some, too. We're thirsty."

The king shuddered.

"水!"国王惊呼
"Water!"He Exclaimed

"水是世界上最危险的东西。"他严厉地说，"糖一碰到水就会融化，把水喝进肚里，你们转眼间就会丧命。"

　　"我们不是糖做的。"唐可儿说，"在我们国家，我们想喝多少水就喝多少。"

　　"Nothing in the world," said he gravely, "is so dangerous as water. It melts sugar in no time, and to drink it would destroy you instantly."

　　"We're not made of sugar," said Twinkle. "In our country we drink all the water we want."

"那也许不假，"国王回答，"但是谢天谢地，在这个天赐的国度里一滴水也没有。但是我们有糖浆，糖浆对健康有益得多。它可以填补你身体里的空隙，凝固后使你变得更结实。"

"可是，喝了糖浆我会更渴的。"小姑娘说，"既然你们没有水，我们就必须抓紧时间，赶快回家了。"

"It may be true," returned the king; "but I am thankful to say there is no drop of water in all this favored country. But we have syrup, which is much better for your health. It fills up the spaces inside you, and hardens and makes you solid."

"It makes me thirstier than ever," said the girl. "But if you have no water we must try to get along until we get home again."

吃完茶点，他们又上了马车，返回城里。路上，六匹糖马却变得烦躁不安，一个劲儿地欢蹦乱跳，那个糖做的赶车人简直没法管住它们。快到宫殿时，一根缰绳断了，说时迟那时快，六匹马突然发疯般地奔走四散。马车撞在一堵高高的糖墙上，碎成了许多片，几个糖人和唐可儿、查宾斯都被抛出来，摔向四面八方。

When the luncheon was over, they entered the carriage again and were driven back towards the city. On the way the six sugar horses became restless, and pranced around in so lively a manner that the sugar coachman could scarcely hold them in. And when they had nearly reached the palace a part of the harness broke, and without warning all six horses dashed madly away. The chariot smashed against a high wall of sugar and broke into many pieces, the sugar people, as well as Twinkle and Chubbins, being thrown out and scattered in all directions.

小姑娘一点儿也没受伤，查宾斯也没有，他落在墙头上，只好从那儿爬下来。可是国王的皇冠断了一个尖角，他坐在地上，愁闷地看着失事的马车。克罗伊老爷——就是那个糖霜男人——一只脚被撞断了。于是大家便都看见了，糖霜下面是一种很像棉花糖的物质。这一发现，肯定会使他不再有资格跻身该国实心糖贵族的阶层了。

The little girl was not at all hurt, nor was Chubbins, who landed on top the wall and had to climb down again. But the king had broken one of the points off his crown, and sat upon the ground gazing sorrowfully at his wrecked chariot. And Lord Cloy, the frosted man, had smashed one of his feet, and everybody could now see that underneath the frosting was a material very like marshmallow—a discovery that was sure to condemn him as unfit for the society of the solid sugar-loaf aristocracy of the country.

不过，受伤最严重的可能要数萨卡琳公主——她的左腿从膝盖处折断了。唐可儿以最快的速度跑到她身边，发现公主竟然望着捡起来的那条断腿，开心地笑着。

　　"快看，唐可儿，"她喊道，"我跟国王大人一样，是实心的！我根本不是空心人，那都是我自己胡思乱想。"

But perhaps the most serious accident of all had befallen Princess Sakareen, whose left leg had broken short off at the knee. Twinkle ran up to her as soon as she could, and found the Princess smiling happily and gazing at the part of the broken leg which she had picked up.

"See here, Twinkle," she cried; "it's as solid as the king himself! I'm not hollow at all. It was only my imagination."

萨卡琳公主摔断了腿

The Princess' Leg Had Broken

"我为你高兴。"唐可儿回答，"可是你腿断了怎么办呢？"

　　"哦，那很容易补好的。"公主说，"我只需要在断的部位抹点糖浆，把两头粘在一起，然后坐下来吹吹风，直到糖浆凝固。不出一小时，我就会变得完好如初。"

　　听了这话，唐可儿很高兴，因为她非常喜欢这位漂亮的糖公主。

　　"I'm glad of that," answered Twinkle; "but what will you do with a broken leg?"

　　"Oh, that's easily mended, " said the Princess, "All I must do is to put a little syrup on the broken parts, and stick them together, and then sit in the breeze until it hardens. I'll be all right in an hour from now."

　　It pleased Twinkle to hear this, for she liked the pretty sugar princess.

第八章
Chapter VIII

经历失控后
After the Runaway

这时，国王来到他们面前，说道："我希望各位没有受伤。"

"我们都没事儿，"唐可儿说，"但我渴得要命。所以，如果陛下不反对的话，我想我们要回家了。"

"当然不反对。"国王回答。

NOW the king came up to them, saying: "I hope you are not injured."

"We are all right," said Twinkle; "but I'm getting dreadful thirsty, so if your Majesty has no objection I guess we'll go home."

"No objection at all," answered the king.

查宾斯一直平静地把破损的车轮辐条和被毁马车的其他碎片装进自己口袋；不过，他和唐可儿一样渴坏了，所以很高兴得知他们马上就要动身回家。

他们跟所有的糖人朋友们告别，感谢糖国王的尊贵款待。脆脆队长和他的士兵把两个孩子护送到拱门，当时他们就是从这里进入糖块城的。

Chubbins had been calmly filling his pockets with broken spokes and other bits of the wrecked chariot; but feeling nearly as thirsty as Twinkle, he was glad to learn they were about to start for home.

They exchanged good-byes with all their sugar friends, and thanked the sugar king for his royal entertainment. Then Captain Brittle and his soldiers escorted the children to the archway through which they had entered Sugar-Loaf City.

回去时没有遇到任何麻烦，不过地道里有的地方太黑了，他们只好摸索着往前走。最后，前面终于有了光亮，几分钟后，他们便爬上那几级石阶，从那道小门挤了出来。

他们的篮子还在原来的地方，下午的阳光温柔地照着周围熟悉的景物，唐可儿和查宾斯都很高兴能再次看到这一切。

They had little trouble in going back, although the tunnel was so dark in places that they had to feel their way. But finally daylight could be seen ahead, and a few minutes later they scrambled up the stone steps and squeezed through the little doorway.

There was their basket, just as they had left it, and the afternoon sun was shining softly over the familiar worldly landscape, which they were both rejoiced to see again.

"钥匙呢？" 唐可儿问
"Where's the Key?" Asked Twinkle

查宾斯关上铁门，锁舌立刻滑入槽中，把铁门牢牢锁上了。

　　"钥匙呢?"唐可儿问。

　　"我本来放在口袋里的，"查宾斯说，"肯定是我从国王的马车里摔出来时给弄丢了。"

Chubbins closed the iron door, and as soon as he did so the bolts shot into place, locking it securely.

"Where's the key?" asked Twinkle.

"I put it into my pocket," said Chubbins, "but it must have dropped out when I tumbled from the king's chariot."

"真糟糕，"唐可儿说，"现在没有人能再进入糖城了。门锁上了，钥匙却在门里。"

"没关系，"男孩说，"我们曾经见过糖块山里的景象，够我们记一辈子了。走吧，唐可儿，我们赶紧回家喝水！"

"That's too bad," said Twinkle; "for now no one can ever get to the sugar city again. The door is locked, and the key is on the other side."

"Never mind," said the boy. "We've seen the inside of Sugar-Loaf Mountain once, and that'll do us all our lives. Come on, Twink. Let's go home and get a drink!"